Squandered Advice

THE GERMAN LIST

ILSE AICHINGER

Squandered Advice

TRANSLATED BY STEPH MORRIS

LONDON NEW YORK CALCUTTA

This publication was supported by a grant from the Austrian
Federal Ministry for Education, Arts and Culture, and the
Goethe-Institut India.

Seagull Books, 2022

First published in German as *Verschenkter Rat* by Ilse Aichinger
© S. Fischer Verlag GmbH, Frankfurt am Main, 1978

First published in English translation by Seagull Books, 2022
English translation © Steph Morris, 2022

ISBN   978 0 8574 2 978 0

British Library Cataloguing-in-Publication Data
A catalogue record for this book is available from
the British Library

Typeset by Seagull Books, Calcutta, India
Printed and bound in the USA by Integrated Books International

Squandered Advice

Ridge

And what would I do
if it weren't for the hunters, my dreams,
climbing down the far side
of the mountains
each morning
in shadow.

Winter Reply

The world is made of stuff
that wants watching,
no eyes left
to see the white fields,
no ears to hear birds whirring
in the branches.
Grandma, where are the lips you need
to taste the grasses,
and who will sniff the sky till it's done,
whose cheeks will rub sore
on the village walls now?
Have we not wound up
in a dark wood?
No, Grandma, it is not dark,
I know. I lived a while
among the kids at its edge,
and nor is it a wood.

Sunday Morning

Love God,
worship him,
serve him
alone.
A rest
at that time,
on the road to the farms,
seen from afar
over the snow.

Marianne

It consoles me
that in those gold nights
a child is asleep.
That her breath strides alongside the forge
and her sun rises early
with the chickens and cockerel
over the damp lawn.

Abroad

Books from strange libraries,
pigeons emboldened.
As if they mattered,
the places we can leave now,
with their raspberry canes,
linen
folding in the wind already,
swapped in silence behind us
while we remain
on the warm backs
of the gardens, stony,
sandy.

A Dedication

I won't be writing to you, any of you,
but I'd find it easy to die with you.
We'd lower ourselves gingerly down from the moons
and take our first rest with the woollen hearts
but by the second we'd reach wolves and raspberry bushes,
the fire which fails to soothe. By the third I'd be
beyond the thin falling cloud with its sparse mosses,
and the poor teeming stars we'd easily pass,
with you in your heaven.

Farm Girl Shortage

Who will keep check on the rocks,
who will hem the grasses,
who fence off the spaces
beyond the roads?
The girls who used spoons
have taken the stones away
in their shoes,
long gone.
Who will help us now,
who will play the sun's
gentle game?
Have we been left alone,
tree by tree?
Or will the shadows,
our friends,
soon creep down from their webs
towards us?

Using Dull Hours

Let the riff-raff
rest in the fields
in the rising mist,
for there's nothing to light your way.
The grotto trains in the hills
are still now,
the beets long dug from the ground,
the children gone.
The flower-weavers are the last
to stay:
They are burning oil.
You can talk to them.

Village Street

The starlings carp in autumn
and sometimes I hear the doors slam twice,
in a dream just once.

Who gave us these pictures,
the red apples
in the charcoal burner's garden,
muddled, but happy to hunker down with us.

Correspondence

If the post came at night
and the insults
were slipped through the door
by the moon
they would look like angels
in their white robes
standing still in the hall.

Rauchenberg

The bridle,
wreaths on the wall,
the shadows' fresh track
shows me the way.

Near the rusting truck,
beside the sunken timbers,
my dearest can bend
better over the roof.

Late

Wood shades
and the candle
lit in the shadows, rust-red,
the wind rushing
down the swathe
drawing the sun away.

Only when
bakery and barn
extend towards their decline
does the sky catch the trunks,
rusting the snow
before the year.

My Father

He was sitting on the bench
when I got there.
The snow rose from the path.
He asked where Laudon's grave was
but I didn't know.

The End of the Unwritten

This way no one will know
how we spluttered,
running over the bridge,
and they won't find out
what lies behind us,
the faint signatures,
guillotined suns.
The hospital lobbies
are quiet.

Near Linz

Me with the day on my heels
and the bumpy country roads.
Listen to that clattering!
Don't catch me up, dear day
but do stay on my heels.

Part of the Question

The water is up high on the square,
air rising as bubbles still,
but what they are singing
cannot reach me now.
The fish circle the steeples.
Answer me this:
should I enter the hill
or the house with the ones
who love me,
and the long view,
every footstep crunching
yet again?
How blackened my land has become,
but deep below
time buckles green.

Winter Dawn

Before the dreams rust and snap
let the lovers climb down,
the tall and the short ones
in their grey coats,
look, those bright tracks, that ice.

The Last Night

And what should come to light
if not the snow trails,
swords down the sides of childhood,
and by the woods
apple trees' limbs
rinsed black by the moon,
the chickens, all counted.

Attempt

Between ladder and north wall,
an afternoon call and warped timber,
scraps of apple and snow,
a connection to be made,
irrevocable.

Sketching Trees

for Eva, Pia, Florian, Julian
and Manuel Aicher.35

Here, now
take these twigs
and take them at their word,
paint them, hang them up,
spread them out,
and let mice at them,
whatever else occurs to you:
calm hands and shaky,
badgers and shoots,
your brothers and sisters'
appeals on behalf of the heavy-hearted,
white needles and red,
everything just as it is
and just as it is not,
snow and lime,
some help, yet no help,
no comfort, yet some comfort.

A Walk

As the world is made of distances,
stairwells and marshes,
and all things bearable are suspect,
you mustn't allow
the magpies beyond your sheds
to fly up briefly, glistening
as they dive on the glistening ponds,
or your smoke still to rise
against the woods.
We'd rather wait
till the golden foxes show up
in the snow.

St Gilgen

Wilting now,
the blossom reveals its lines,
the grain of wood
on derelict bathing huts,
cracks in the majolica
on shaky shelves,
unseen,
tyre tracks at the bend
and the hasty departure,
shadows of branches at the time
they were all asleep:
the water's long gone games
at midday.

Hay

Hay,
hay in the children's barns where
it's as easy
to burn
as to lose yourself for ever.
Bales of hay,
hay in the fields,
hay as the letters combined
just so from the lethal range
of possibilities,
this way round
and no other.
Hay, which flies in the wind,
and catches on spindly stubble,
always split from the others,
waiting for snow,
which will rob it of the sky,
its soft, immobile likeness.
The certainty it offers no comfort,
but still the cheers,
hay, snow, an end.

Card Game

Forgetting dark recesses,
faces
and the gold under the wall,
we leave everything where it is,
the swing and the tin men,
the patterns which made us go blind,
and a rhino under the kitchen bench
warmed by candlelight.

Bobinger's Lament

My friends are dispelled.
I lost them
among the leaves and branches.
Who will resolve this picture,
who will pull their pale forms
out of the rain for me again,
who will help them catch cloud caps,
who will help me turn the sundial?

Attersee

Sketch of the fish which died in the depths,
thrown on the white wall at twelve,
snatched from the white wall at twelve
by the sexton, who came to lock the doors.
No one saw them.

Breitbrunn

Our childhood days
incline towards
our later days.
And if you ask about home
they say, all those who stay:
the grass has grown.
But nothing
about how the winding ways
down the hill
rose up and sighed.
Before they die
the priests move
to another village.

The Start of Winter

Nothing else in the cabinet.
The soldiers who died at midday
sleep easier beneath glass.
It's thanks to the way the wind blows
that the grasses shrank back
and withered,
that the frames fitted,
the autumns sealed.
Where did my kite fly, how swiftly?
How did that happen? Did it sink,
flaming red, to bed down
on your house?

Self-built

I want to leave my village
without words
and swing through
the snow only,
free against the fences.
From up in my attic
I want to watch the jaguars,
hear the wolves whistle.
The sun leapt away
but the children
had help
with the dandelion harvest.
Room for the king!

Instruction

Take desires.
At its edges
cast the earth in wax,
forming ridges.
Peel away.
And with these hollow roses,
some claim,
we have new saviours,
heroes, protesters,
outriders.
Friends, they say.

Cautious

All of them open,
the rabbis' cabinets
and the bees' huts,
in a bookcase resistant
target ships,
escaping the coast,
caves and sore beasts.
Your knees tremble,
Jonathan, when you jump
and risk it ahead.
But do jump, they can hold on to you.
Pop violets in your buttonhole.
The carpenters are exposed
in each rock.

To Myself

I wanted to talk of living there that long,
of bowling and red wooden skittles
on the terrace, of the views beyond.
I wanted to repeat the cries of the men on the ice
precisely, and how the skittles clattered too.
And the windowsill-flowers I wanted to describe,
how they grew to the sun.
What did I do?

Two Sites, Combined

How should I identify the days?
By the green bishops' robes,
saints' visits,
and a brief peace?

Where the grass bakes
the sleepers corrode
in the dark bakeries.
Who will keep my heaven
for me?

Winter Drift

I let the hunting bugles
flush me out
of my bolt holes,
out to the red dawn
beneath the snow,
to the yellowing grass.

With my hands
now I can reach
the Ancients' vows,
who draw me swiftly up,
fetch me
the convoluted moon.

Winter, Painted

And in white jackets
in the snow, the Austrians.
Let's look up
and spot their tracks
in the finch song,
in the peaks.
The Mount of Olives
paint is deepening green
from the walls,
the whispering roofs of barns.
The shadows will never
shift as gently as today.

Simple Choice

I hear the voices,
that read *Robinson Crusoe* aloud,
that make do with these walls,
that choose grief,
heavenly handmaid.
I sink into the looks,
covered in dust now,
that can lightly survey me
with the blink of an eyelid.

Our Woman

Our woman
is a member of the moaning brigade.
She rides her bike to the barn
to bemoan the living.
The buttercups light her up, the brook.
When she shuts her eyes
the quarry flies by red.

Into the Village

I don't trust this peace,
those neighbours, rose hedges,
that whispered word.
I heard
that they tie their skins to a snare,
that they tip their benches before winter.
Their whoops soared,
ready for sleep,
through the school and church buildings
up and away.
Who still expects the birds
that stay,
the smoke crossing the short grass?

Out of the Village

The village stretches off.
Part with it,
dug up and tired,
leave it lying
as it is, leaden,
the gutters free, dry,
blocked by the sun,
nothing up in the sky.
The last cockroach
to get to safety
before the flood
without Noah
scuttles into a puddle.
The new toll collector laughs.

Florestan

Now I'd like to
catch you
in corridors
Brother,
drive you
under the snow.
I'd like to show you
crossings
and the spots to
stop for a moment.
I'd like to shoo you
from bright plazas
so you fly far out
and find your way
away to me,
our wreath
by night.

Three Kings Rhyme

We come from Persian lands afar.
The bishop's mitre has lifted
plane-tree gardens
swiftly into the picture.
Sunburn has blackened us
and strung us between the casks
and the countries of Carniola,
Gorizia, and Gradiška,
also the white swings.
We are called moors,
because Carinthia was lost.
Master give us work then.
Master, what are you called?

Reading

The reading matter is green,
falls through square panes,
and lies on the quarry tiles
in the porch
far from the rhododendrons
but not till afternoon.

A Moth's Name

Lourdes comes down,
a poor girl,
and again she leaves
the blue mountains be
and gathers kindling
in her dark cap
and takes the roundabout way,
catching sheep and catching water
and sweeps past your blank hedges
on her own.

Wedding Procession

We reached the tree in Holnis
and beneath it
found lots of soft children, asleep
with eyes
wide open, dreaming.
Cherries glinting in the hay
between barn doors,
blue crinkles,
old wheels,
shadows still of distant whoops,
long since rolled inland,
who said, to sea?

Thirteen Years

Far afield, the feast of tabernacles,
the shine on chestnuts
lined on the summer house sill.
And still in the room
the candle,
the world's religions.

Desert dust beneath a bike tyre.
From noon today
dusk comes sooner.
The comrades
and a green grave,
Raisa.

In the evening we'll be back.
Nevermore will we be back.

Gonzagagasse

The sky fed the flames escaping the lofts.
It bred them, it taught them to burn, enthralled them
along the wooden struts on the bridges.
All the while the salt boats calmly floated by,
tolls were taken, tariffs paid,
pigeons grew in numbers.
In front of the cobbler's hopscotch flourished.
There they leapt, wrapped in dark coats
for those spring nights are icy, square to square,
sticking within the slabs, towards the chalk curve.

No Years

Philippshof, branches,
dust, as it was summer,
and courage.
What's left gives pause for thought,
and what's not left
same thing once more.
Rosemary has a colour,
and has it yet.
The heads rounded, angled, smooth
and other
or is that not a word,
to describe the world,
the sky's borders up above the ramps?
Joy is one thing
and is it again
and will be it once more
in the villages
where they guard consent,
with their glass fishes
woods waving down,
piers built of branches,
storms and courage.

The Architect's Orders during Construction of Prinz Eugen Strasse

Start with
a wide strip of wind.
At its side plant that stag's horn sumac,
don't ignore the pigeons,
and soon enough, I swear,
the dust will rise
from your dreams.
As these clouds
battle to the brighter ones in the sky
you'll find the design,
you'll know the plan.

Trieste

In the shadows dropped by leaves I saw
the shapes of armour-plated lands.
The birds came to me countless
from the sun,
taught me the art of tying bows
over the folded sea
and one of them settled
on my ribs
and discussed me,
and at the pigeon grottos
also my star.

Wish

To learn silence
from curtailed stays,
from the dim timbers,
the unexploited gaps,
from the girls in their white frocks,
columns of dust supporting temples,
from doors in the trembling mirror.

For My Grandmother

The double doors
onto Modenapark,
the question
about origins,
about religions,
the street, Salesianergasse,
Major Schulz's wife,
His Excellency Zwitkowitsch,
the terror,
the humility,
the subjection,
Miss Belmont,
the sanctuary,
the strange hallway,
the gate,
which burst open,
the mad dog.
Don't worry,
he's white,
still little, and
he's running past.

Middling Verdict

So if you travel to Turkey,
says my grandmother,
and die there,
it is of course
in a Turkish cemetery that you'll
be buried.

Through and Through

We were only ever
threaded through briefly here
but ever since
they have kept the eye from us
like camels.

Marking Time

It's turned twelve,
twelve and the picture of the picture on the wall,
and the frozen jolts.
It will turn on from twelve
although it can't go on
turning on from twelve this way.
It will turn one.

Counted Out

The day on which you
ended up in the ice with no shoes,
the day on which
the two calves
were sent to slaughter,
the day on which I
shot myself in the left eye,
but no longer,
the day on which
it said in the butchery newsletter
life goes on,
the day on which it went on.

Obituary

Give me the cloak, Martin,
but get out of the saddle first
and leave your sword where it is.
Give me the whole thing.

Words of Encouragement to a Man
Who Lay in Bed for Twenty-Three Years
Then Got Up

Those seconds
the length of the bedside,
be glad,
really do be glad,
I mean it, in the name
of the town,
Newcastle upon Tyne,
of the sheep-shearing
you so gallantly
sat through,
of the new breed
which places you
above the pigs,
way above,
of the pretty whistle,
from Scotland,
to and fro,
don't stand stone still,
be glad.

Sidelong View

Nothing further.
Floodlight
on the fur curing workshop,
the burnt gladioli,
the fellows' lamps.
We're cared for well
by the bright Dutch,
we wear spurs
on our high heels,
and snow to the lynx chapel,
embellishment, green, demolished,
further, nothing.

Abandoned Manoeuvre

It was long since white.
The buildings tempted
dread from the future.
Baltimore was far off
and all that lot,
Orion and the grass.
From what mid-point
did we steal the start,
peeling off
and tearing holes
only to be called
the names we liked,
blue or otherwise,
swearing and forswearing
enclosures in that fall,
having them crash too,
bringing them along with us?
Now they reflect,
all of them, even those rescued,
wings, winging, hindrances,
and white it is.

The Birthplace

for Monika Schoeller

Perhaps
in the view of the vineyards
where generosity sprouts.
Finding the Salesianergassen
springing out of hedges,
ever fresh finds,
essential the expectation
of the unpredicted,
foreseeing the unforeseeable,
devotion, discretion, deed.

Summer Party

I ask myself
why you relish names,
Gaspard, Leberecht, Sonnenrand?
And tell myself
it's because although they might be missing
I still wouldn't let you
grieve.

March

The grey cows step
over the roofs and down.
The trees' shade
keeps pace with the graves,
shredded scraps of sun.
The women in the windows
admit soon
it will rain.
Assuming of course
we are in agreement.

March Request to the Garden

Stay a panther,
black-haired,
blotched and hungry
for Easter Tuesdays,
streaks of rain
and rosary rules,
for those too
that ease,
for the cast-off winnings
from children's raffles,
the contents of
sweet, hollow epistles.
Stay this way,
wet and raging,
as you are now,
ready,
from the first kitten
right to the whetstone
and the long boundary,
to swallow it
all,
and all its contrasts.
Stay this way,
stay hungry
for us.

After

Going out
to the spot
which is quiet
in the sun
which today
has cut that racket,
that old swagger.
Finding out,
now finding out,
where they ran to,
who were
bold and gentle here,
in which shapes,
choirs, machinations
they cannot be found.

Chinese Goodbye

We will lie down today,
doubly down.
Should you wish to wake us
best be gentle,
best take care of your voice,
as well as your heart,
for both are precious.

Old View

I've got used to this window
and the snow falling through my eyes,
but who followed the lost ones
through the open garden gate,
who sealed what was there,
the water butt
and the moon as moon,
all the frozen grasses?
Who swung before morning,
making the ropes creak?
Who places a wax hand
on the kitchen window,
who settled in white
and absorbed me, myself?

Utterly

The lads with the death certificates
have vanished.
They rode out of the bazaars at speed
on former horses.
They are gone.

All we can contemplate is
the Saurians' guile
and how they shrunk
down to our scale,
the signs of the upheaval
and their sheer end,
tips and hints,
and their decline.

Thought Up

Once the tortures are bunched
I'll head to Bayonne
and slip through the mesh
which I mean
and hear the plaster creak,
which I wanted,
how I wanted,
but won't stroke it,
and as long as I want.

Earmarked for the End

But when the court sits
I'll be miles from Bayonne,
miles from *bonnes vacances*.
Will they find me?

Snow People

I don't mix lightly with
the strangers made of snow,
coals, carrots and sticks.
I won't touch them
while they still gaily flaunt it,
some with more faces
than the one.
When the coals
and the carrots then fall,
buttons, strips of buttons,
red lip ribbons,
I watch stiffly
and without a sound.
I do not rush to assist.
Their Milanese may be
nicer than mine.
It mustn't come to light.
Silence then,
till this light has softly
stolen them
and everything obscured
between Milanese
and Milanese,
and then me too.

In What Name

The name Alissa,
the name Inverness,
brought here
when, and from which
desert edges,
by which orders,
of monks, of nuns,
lengthways or sideways,
and to where, where not,
as if tenable,
as if wasteful,
with walls in circles
in winter sun,
in graves torn open,
ramparts, cradles
with fire, ringlets?
Oh names, names,
at least I'm not christened
either of you,
and am not guilty.

Photofit

Moby Dick,
Rabbi Fingerhut
has drowned,
has died,
gone.
He had yellow eyes
and a large mouth,
dark regalia
packed onto him.
Moby Dick,
Rabbi Fingerhut.
Tell Ahab too,
and the others,
the helmsmen
and the harpooners
and tell them soon.
Pass it on,
don't forget.

Small Sum

No lasso thrown
from the *falaises*
to Mill Hill,
no link between
the boating devotees of Napoleon.
They are waiting still,
none of them moved to the madness
he called for,
none of them along
on the old path over the cliffs
to heaven,
and the Flaubertian coterie
still not yet ready
to offer support.
No flares detected,
between me and myself,
just something admitted on enquiry:
it is getting dark now.

No Bundle

Prove
and escape to the proof,
compliant stone, no fist
butting in,
and when the old woman
steps on her hair
no movement,
and when she
drinks her caustic soda
don't approach,
don't take a thing,
escape again,
don't die,
even if the path dies,
and when the wreathes
hit your temples
at the end, without end,
and mount
on your skulls, be glad
you've come that far.

New Covenant

The sun is pushing in front of me
into my peace,
jumping, shoving, with childish gestures,
won't wait for me.
And so I am leaving
this peace,
this dear peace
for the shade
and my dear pigs
the only fierce and fearless ones
who know to drown
in our dull water
as commanded,
as in the commandments,
who no sun can catch
and corrupt,
who stick around, what's more, after the end.
My kings.

Thirty-One

I'll happily let myself go
and take the thirty silver coins along
around my neck
if I'm handed them,
so we can swing,
we thirty-one,
so I can hear them jangling
in their jute sack,
on and out of the world,
so when my tongue stiffens,
I can catch the voice
with my bare ears
telling you,
start over!
So I am cheerful then.

Ire and Fire

I'll insist on you two
when the doomsday judge comes.
I'll ask him why
he didn't wake me
that July,
where he was
when both the wild ones drowned,
my red-pelts, and yours,
one in hope,
the other not.

Day After Tomorrow

The final reports
from the villages
shift with little effort
where air and cables graze.
Who knows who left whom?
A voice hangs up
and is free
again and gone.

Daytime

A calm June day
smashes my bones,
upends me,
flings me to the gate
sticks those pins to me,
the ones in the colours
yellow, white and silvery-white,
won't fail me
for anyone,
lets go only the fool's hat,
my favourite,
strangles me
with its latest noose,
as long as I'm still breathing.
Stay, dear day.

Timely Advice

Firstly,
you must believe
that it's day
when the sun rises.
But should you not believe it
say yes.
Secondly,
you must believe,
believe with all your strength,
that it's night
when the moon shines.
But should you not believe it
say yes
or nod your head compliantly.
They accept that too.

Options

Whether
when I brush the mirrored wardrobe
with my left shoulder
I assist a perjurer
like someone who dies.
Whether
when I turn out the light at my place
someone else,
someone in Touraine,
someone in decline,
sees their next step again.
Whether
when I go to bed at our place
among sick stems,
someone else,
among quite different
healthy stems,
goes out into the fields
but with a light, strong rope
in his hand.

Foundling

Shoved under the snow,
never mentioned to the angels,
no bronze, no shelter,
never presented to the fairies,
solely concealed in caves,
their symbols swiftly erased
from the forest map,
a mad fox
bites her and warms her
shows her the first affection till,
trembling and tortured,
it heads off to die.
Who will help the child?
The mother,
with her old worries?
The hunters,
with their falsified maps?
The angels,
with their warm wing-feathers,
but without a remit?
No sound,
no pulse in the air,
no pad on the ground.

So come back,
you mad old hero,
drag yourself back to her,
bite her, scratch her,
warm her, if your preying paws are warm still,
for aside from you no one will come,
rest assured.

Belonging

My black beasts,
who I see grazing,
who graze away for me
into the wood, the algae,
my creatures,
who stop me
from being,
who ride apart
what's ahead,
who know it,
for they're mine
and nothing more.

Untimely

You have placed no stone for me,
to deepen our old grief,
left no candle to dread
or any dread to make it brighter,
or even that scrap of sadness,
all the stars demand.
You're busy with your foundling
and I haven't yet found
the waxwork girls,
stiller even
than Jesus in the crib,
not yet.

Brief Lullaby

Rouen
be with you,
the apple sugar,
the haughty sun
free of aggression,
let it be with you,
Rouen, Rouen.

Request

You needn't shield me
from wrathful gods,
from a wrathful God,
for I won't come to you in fear.
The wheels on the white hill turn.
Homer is slumped in his corner.
Wake him.
Wake him for me
with your last laugh
so that I hear you
when I walk among the wheels
and he sings.

One 4th of March

Nothing can get a grip.
The fledglings are running barefoot in the wind.
The shoemakers have flown the nest.
The plans were carted off in daylight, yesterday.
Join us on the long meadow
and the first of us
to find seven beaks on their face
and the plague in their throat
before we lie down to sleep
is the winner.

Loose Rungs

with thanks to Heinrich Böll

I fling all the shotguns
into the corn
and walk across them gingerly
so I don't otherwise trample a thing.
On this silent ladder
I make my way out
to the edge of the field.

Response

In Delhi, when you die
you cannot fall.

Günter Eich

put it behind you,
Delhi,
reclaim
the falling sickness
set your sights on it,
Delhi,
slowly follow
the squalid bands of travellers
and so
abandon your travels
in silence and in every sense
and even if no longer
visible

To a Young Tanner

There a thrush egg,
and there a deathbed.
Things are linked
along this scale.
Fare well, lively tanner,
son of a tanner,
grandson,
fare well in your skins,
stay fresh within them
as long as you have no fear,
then leave.

Squandered Advice

I

Your first chess book,
Ibsen's letters,
take it on board
if you can,
there, take it,
or would you rather
drive the leaf sweepers
from your grass
and bring in
Ibsen's goats,
as white, as radiant?
There are goats and there are Ibsen's goats.
There is the sky and there is a Spanish Opening.
Listen up child,
there is tinplate, they say,
there is the world.
Check that they aren't lying.

II

And ask them
what this foreign thorax
is doing in the garden,
already stone still,
the first this spring,
in the bramble patches.
Mice
and the wall
water beats against
for us.
Ask what good it does the garden,
if it needs our garden,
if the garden
needs it.

III

And
we were told something
about periods of time.
Was this about periods, certain times,
about period times, about time, period,
or none of the above?

In One

And if I had no dreams
I wouldn't be another person.
I'd be the same without dreams.
Who would call me home?

A NOTE ON THE TEXT

In a varied literary career which encompassed all genres Ilse Aichinger's *Squandered Advice* (*Verschenkter Rat*) was her sole poetry collection, although the very short prose of her *Kurzschlüsse* (Short Circuits) is sometimes seen as prose poetry. The collection was first published in 1978, and included poems written from the 1950s to the 1970s. They were arranged by her according to thematic and poetic affinity, not chronologically, and no dates were given. Instead the composition of the book as a whole was prioritized. For the second, final edition, in 1991, on which this translation is based, she added some poems written later, inserting them into the previously ordered sequence where she felt they fitted poetically.